# The Wind
# Has Many Faces

# THE WIND HAS MANY FACES

## A Book of Minute Meditations

### by

### Joan Hutson

A PRIORITY EDITION

Abbey Press
St. Meinrad, Indiana 47577
1974

First published, 1974
© 1974 by Joan Hutson
Library of Congress Catalog Card Number: 74-78724
ISBN: 0-87029-031-2
Printed in the U.S.A.

Abbey Press
St. Meinrad, Indiana 47577

# Contents

CATHEDRAL

```
                    C
                    a
                    t
                    h
              Cathedral
                    d
                    r
                    a
                    l
                    O
                  God
                 come
               into the
            deserted mar-
           ketplace of my
          soul and help me
        throw away the empty
          crates that life has
        loaded in without dis-
        cretion. Each has been
       torn open, and found empty.
      I don't like to see them lying
    around anymore. They point so hurt-
      fully to the fact that I have tried every-
```
thing to still the restlessness that so often threatened to sunder
my joints. I've invited everything, everyone, into my bustling marketplace because their jostling, raucous laughter, and incessant
talk distracted me, kept me from thinking. But at last I couldn't
tolerate the din. It cramped me, crowded me, and my eternal unrest
shouted: "Leave, leave everything, everyone." Now I am here alone.
Empty wrappers, empty crates to remind me of my past busy existence.
The marketplace of my soul is deserted. O God, I cry to you through
the intractable reaches of time, please, please, make of me . . . a cathedral

LEAF

I
com-
pare
my life to an
autumn leaf—a
leaf at the mercy of
the wind. With no set di-
rection of its own, it wanders, wanders, wanders. Where,
O leaf, is your destiny? One day
you walk the winding country road;
one day you swirl around the street-
vendor's feet. One day you are free
to skip across open fields, the next
day you are caught in the hollow of
a tree. It hurts me to see you
without destination of your
own. You have no goals
of your own, you must let
the circumstance of the
wind decide your fate.
I don't know why
this disturbs me
so, O leaf . . .
unless your
aimless
life re-
minds
me
so
of
me.

NO ROOM

I
re-
member
O Lord, a
weatherworn
stable that once
became a cathedral,
how coarse,   splintered
boards trembled in awe, never
having been more than a stable
before,   a   rough-hewn   manger,
standing   breathlessly   still,   never
having been a chalice before, rough
swaddling   clothes,   now   altar   cloths,
a sputtering lantern, now a vigil light,
clumsy cattle, unlearned shepherds, now wor-
shippers. Mary, in shadowed light, looks lovingly

down on God's            new redeeming Light.
Joseph, looking           at  the leaning walls,
wishes  he could          have provided a palace,
yet realizes that          the Presence of a King
makes  a  stable  a       palace.   The  Infant  looks
about  at  the  world     He came to save: a world that
closed its door to Him    even before He was born. Mary,
why  is  your  joy inter-  mingled with sorrow tonight? "Because I fear hearts may be  like the inn . . . with no room for Him."

TELESCOPE

Sorrow loses its
power to shatter
me if I but gather
it together and lift
the sad parcel to my
ever-caring God. His
tears mingle with mine.
Someday, when they have
done their work on my soul,
He will dry them. But until
the day He does dry the tears,
I will look through them to Him.
Tears are like a telescope; I can
see farther through them. I can see
back to Bethlehem's cold when an Infant's
tear rolled down a cold cheek and warmed
it. I can see back to Calvary's heat when
a grown Man's tear streaked down a fevered
cheek and cooled it. And I can see ahead to
a day when my tears will be tears of joy when
He says to me: "Come enter the home of My Father."

THE AGED

I just came                    from a
home for the aged. I     saw men, women,
waiting to die with pallid, tired hearts. Hope,
drained from eyes;  far too many empty days
had drained the reservoir of anticipation, far too
many days of no one coming to lighten an hour.
The tick, tock, of their last hours has no accompani-
ment. Hands that didn't even know me, grasped mine,
just for a momentary completion     of a human circuit to someone. The flicker of       light in low-
voltage eyes, showed the circuit      was completed. Sometimes their sentences
dropped unfinished, as they realized
no one was really         interested,
their hands cold,        maybe because
no fuel of human kind-     ness had been
fed into the furnace of     their aging hearts.
They, who are so close to     returning to You,
must ache with the poor fare-     well their world
gives—indifference.

TO GOD

A
saint
is one
who knows why he was born. His whole life is a flaming arrow,
directed at a Divine Target.  As he progresses through life, he
G       allows nothing to cling to him that would merely slacken his speed.
GOD   But he is not so concerned with his own arriving that he is oblivious
D       to those around him. If, to help them, he delays his own progress,
he rejoices in this blessed detainment, for he wants the target to
be met by all.  Never is his eye allured to lesser targets.  His
flight
will
hit.

The ancient philosopher Seneca said, "To be happy, add not to your possessions, but subtract from your desires." One should learn to ask, when tempted to add one more accumulation, one more centrifugal activity to his life, "Is it necessary?" First, I will simplify my material life, lighten my environment, strip away the superfluous. Then, I will simplify my relations to others. Keep relationships light and unencumbered, learn to unify myself into a more singular person, so that the inward man and the outward man is one. Learn to keep the door to my heart open, so I am approachable by those who really need me, but not to throw it wide open. Living today tends to fragmentation and disintegration. William James has a German word to describe modern harassed living. *Zerrissenheit*— meaning torn-to-pieceshood. O Lord, help me avoid it by simplified living, with One Reason for everything I do: You!

**WALLS**

So many
of us
build walls
that shut out not
only people, but
You, my God. It
is true, if we don't tear
down the walls, and let
love in and out, we may
not cry as much, for love
does bring pain. But walls crush us
in time. They close in closer and
closer. Sunlight shadowed out, we
wither, lose vitality, and find we are the only
plant in the garden, and have no reason for trying to bloom anymore. We reach no one; no one
reaches us. Our walls have made a tomb.

BABY

I saw a nursery
B   full of newborn
A     babies, babies
B       fragrantly fresh
Y      from the hand of God,
the aura of heaven
still on them. All
have the same en-
vironment now, white and sterilized.　Within a
week, each will have been already molded to a new
environment. Some will hear Your name, O Lord,
whispered in a lullaby of prayer.　Some
will hear Your name, O Lord, shouted in an
angry curse. Some will know that Your
love covers all like a warm mantle;

others          will
shiver in       the naked-
ness for       never
know-          ing You.

CLOUD

I learned a lesson today
from Your clouds, O Lord. I watched a
   billowy white cloud outlined in luminous white.
      I watched the wind push it, crowd it in with other clouds.
      It lost its brilliance, turned darker and darker.
   Lightning flickered faintly through it; thunder answered softly;
then brighter lightning and louder thunder. Then the cloud
poured itself down onto the land in large raindrops. Thirsty
earth drank, panting animals cooled. The sky had now
      turned into a lukewarm gray. The cloud was completely
         lost in the mass. The cloud, once so unique, so proud
         of its majestic brilliance, became a nothing,
            submissive to the will of God. And I know
               that unless I, too, am willing to be a
               nothing, I will never be anything
                  in the eyes of my Creator.

DIVINE LIGHT

Oh,
Lord,
move
Your holy light
in a little closer
that I might better
discern Your
holy will.

o

o

o

I am so engulfed
in an endless night
of bewilderment, in-
decision, and unrest.
With one divine breath,
blow away these clouds
of uncertainty, so that
the clear light of Your
holy will may pierce the
mists of doubt and be-
come clear to me. Make my
way so clear that not a hint
of doubt remains as to what
Your will is for me. You
said, "Follow Me," but I have
lost sight of Your direction
for me. Pierce the mist that
I might see where you lead . . .

WORDS

Words, why are you so ineffective when I try to reach God or people?
My feelings are strong, but words break down midstream. Or they
burst forth like a scattered group of birds losing solidarity
by flying loose. Often silence says more than words, reaches
deeper into the heart than words, raises to higher heights
than words. casts to lower depths than words. I remember one of
Your silences, O Christ, when the world cried over and
over again two words: "Crucify Him, Crucify Him, Crucify Him . . ."

A WILD ROSE

I picked
a wild rose.
I studied it carefully
and it seemed to
say to me:   "Would you believe
X     that the Hand that
fashioned the softness
X  of me, also shaped the hard
thorns you see on my branches?"
X

X

X

Could it be He did this     X
to show how closely related
joy is to pain , so closely   X
related that both are
nourished by the same root?  X
X            To find the rose
you may have to feel the pain
X     X     of the thorn. To find joy
X     you may have to feel the pain
X   X     of sorrow.

X   X   X   X

The rose slowly wilted
in my hand. The thorn remained
fresh and sharp. Thus the rose
gave me another lesson as it
slowly died: Joy is shorter-
lived than pain.

X

X

X

X

REST

My God, teach
me to live in
simplicity, a
simplicity that
reduces every-
thing to You.
When I awaken in the morning, may I see the day before me
only as an opportunity to serve You in the most perfect way.
Help me to say no to a world that calls me to frivolous ways.
All ways are frivolous that do not lead to You. When I go to
sleep at night, may I see the night before me only as a restful
gift from You,
a rest that will
mercifully blot
out the times I
disappointed You
during the day.
And with the new
day that dawns
tomorrow, may I
begin with a clean
slate, with all
of today's mark-
ings fully erased!

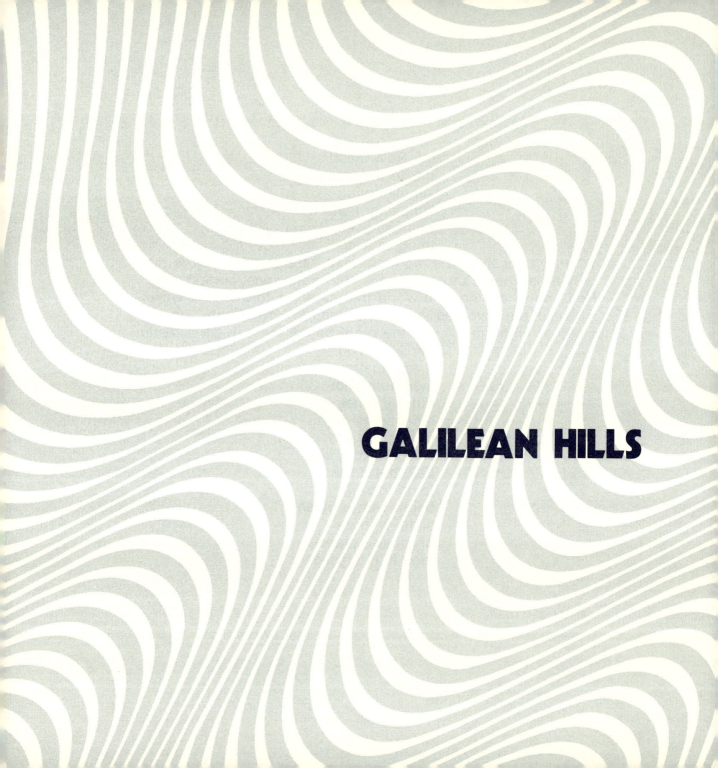

GALILEAN HILLS

                    A
                    soul
                    that feels
                    no just anchorage
                    anywhere in this world,
                    a soul that is always standing
                    on the periphery of belonging, will
                    understand Christ's words: "The foxes have dens,
                    the birds of the air have nests; but the Son of
                    Man has nowhere to lay His head." The Galilean sun warmed and
                    tanned Your divine Face during the day, my Lord, but what did You
                    have to keep You warm at night? You spent Yourself on mankind all day,
                    and at night the world did not afford You a place to rest. Blessed be the
                    sweet smelling hay of the fields which may have softened your bed of earth.
                    Blessed be the rough, rugged trees that slowed down the night winds. Blessed
                    be the deep blue coverlet of sky to which You faced in prayer.
                    Blessed be the stars which etched Your Father's world in silver.

BASIN OF FORGIVENESS

Sometimes, God, I cannot forgive others. I know that You said:
"Forgive us our trespasses as we forgive those who trespass
against us," as You prayed to the Father. Your words
jolt me when I can't find it within me to fully forgive.
I remember You, O Son of God, how You with great
tenderness and love knelt down before one who
had already sold You, and washed his feet,
washing away dust that was clinging to
his feet from the treacherous steps
he had just taken to sell You to
the enemy. My Lord, how could
You? And in juxtaposition I ask
myself, "How could you not forgive anyone
anything as you remember that basin of water."

THE BIRDS

Deep
in the blue-
green shadows of an
evergreen tree is cradled
a bird's nest. The
pine boughs cup
protecting fingers
over it. The sun breathes
on it warmly while afternoon breezes
sway a lullaby. Love dwells there. I
feel it in the mother bird's warm
loving wing; I feel it in the
trusting faces of her young. I
think that You, too, Christ, must
have witnessed this love, for You spoke
of Yourself in contrast: "The birds of the
air have nests, but the Son of Man has nowhere to lay
His head." You slept in open fields; You listened to the
quiet calls of the birds to one another. You saw each bird return
at nightfall
to his own
nest while
You had a
different
hillside each
night.

THE
BIRDS

INSTRUMENT

I visited a
famous guitar-
ist, and as we
talked I noticed
his guitar lean-
ing against a
chair. It looked
like any guitar,
and it added
nothing to
life in its mute-
ness. I looked
at the guitarist's
hands clasped to
gether on the table
between us. They
looked like any other hands
and they added nothing to life in
their inertness. Then the guitarist
picked up the guitar, stirring notes filled
the air, and I experienced the greatness as
instrument and talent flowed together into magnificent melody.
And I thought          of You, God,
as the skillful        player, and I
thought of me as       the instrument.
If I were willing to be used by Your skillful
hands I could be the instrument that brings
Your stirring notes into a world that
so much needs divine melody.

NIGHT

O night,
fall down swiftly on this day
that seemed too long;
with your shadowed soft breath,
wrap me in your dark;
let my tired mind rest in twilight's
embrace. O night, you are my friend;
you silence day's demands; o night,
you take the heights, o night, you take
the depths, and blend them all together
so that neither seems severe. You
neutralize grief with memory of joy.

O night, erase all cares as you shadow my soul in the hands of God.

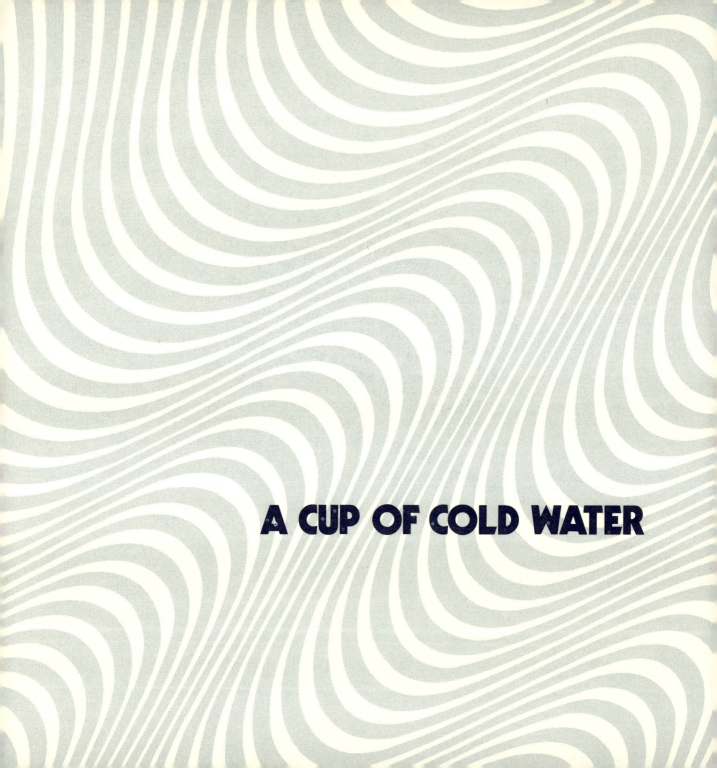

# A CUP OF COLD WATER

Christ, as sure as You walked to Calvary,
You walk our streets today. And I think the
walk to Calvary may have been easier for You.
The people around You then did not know that
You were the Son of God. We do. We won't come under
that mantle of forgiveness that says:        "Father, forgive them, they do not know what            they are doing."
We saw You in countless faces today,        some weary, toil-
worn, unloved.   Their needs did not        impress us much.
Oh, we know what You said, "Whatso-         ever you do to
the least of My brothers, that you do        unto Me," but we
are waiting for bigger opportunities to come along. We don't want
to just listen to others' problems, smile, care, encourage. We want
to do bigger things so that we can see the good we have done,
and so that You can see the good we
have done.   But still, You did say:
"Whoever gives a cup of cold water to
drink in My name shall not lose his
        reward." A cup of water . . .
an attentive ear . . . a loving smile . . .

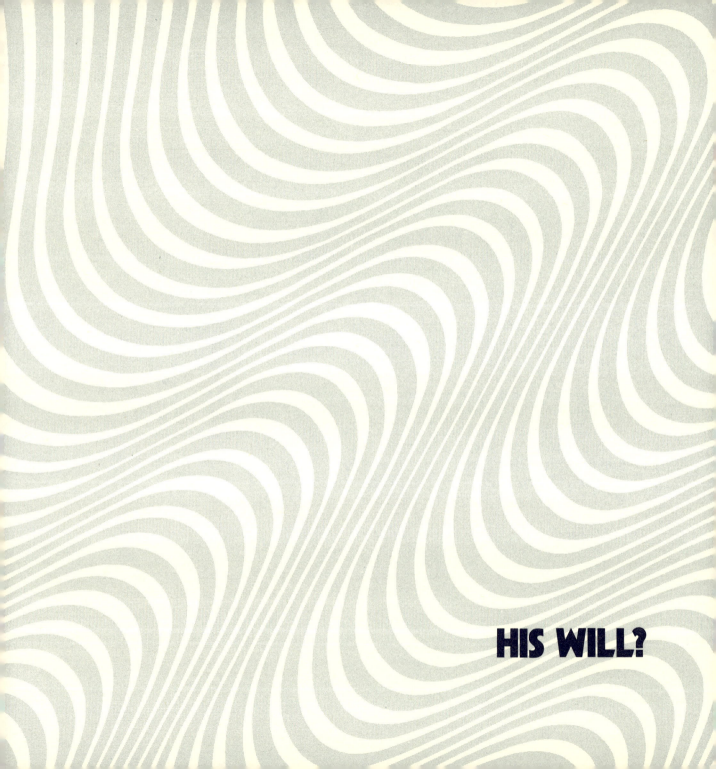

HIS WILL?

So often, O Lord, I am not certain what Your
will is in the decisions I am called upon to
make in a day. Could it be that I don't listen
for Your direction? Knox said: "All our lives,
he but asks that we should steadily listen to
his voice. May he give you the silence of heart
that will listen." And Carlyle said:
"Do but hold your tongue for one day, and
on the morrow how
much clearer are
your purposes and
duties, what wreck
and rubbish have
the mute workmen
within you swept
away . . . " I will
be more certain of
Your will, if I
listen for it:
"God has things
to tell us which
will enlighten us.
We must wait for
Him to speak. No
one will rush into
a physician's
office, rattle
off all the symptoms,
And then dash away without waiting for
a diagnosis. It is every bit as stupid
to ring God's doorbell, and then run
away. The Lord hears us more readily
than we suspect; it is our listening
that needs to be improved. When people
complain that
their prayers
are not heard,
what often has
happened is
that they
did not wait

to hear His
answer," says
Sheen.
Ssshhhhhhhh,
my soul . . .

OMNIPRESENCE

God, like
a litany,
is repeated
over and over
again in His
creation. Do
you recognize the fragrance of Him in the fragile wild rose?
Do you see the delicateness of His stroke in the painted butterfly
wings? Do you experience His silence between the still leaves
of a tree?
Do you feel
His gentle
ways in the
soft falling
rain? Do you
see His per-
fection
in the way He
taught the
blackbird to
build his nest?
Do you see His
respect for free
will in the way
He gives strength
to the hand of
the writer,
even when he
is writing
God is dead.

THE CLOCK

The
clock
has a
restless
beat. It seems
to hurry the moments
with hasty breaths. It
makes me want to
fill my moments—
full. The moments
I waste slip
through my fingers
as easily as pearls
slip from a broken
necklace. Sometimes
everything I do
seems a waste;
nothing I sow seems
to have reaping value
at harvest time. I
glean the fields, and
my hands are empty
still. I don't want

to
waste the moments You give
me, Lord, but so often, I don't
know how to fill them. I sometimes
ask You, but You know how silent You
can be.  So little of what I do could
ever be weighed on Your scales. Will
you weigh smiles, words of encour-
agement, little acts of charity?—
because I fear that is all I
will  ever  have  to give
You.

SOLITARY

Many
trees are
growing close
together here with-
in talking distance of
one another. In the morn-
ing, tree awakens tree as the
morning breezes sway one into another
in a caress of touching, talking leaves.
They shade each other from a scorching noon sun,
and they huddle together at night to sing vespers. Off
a distance stands a lone tree . . . very, very alone. Never
does it feel the loving touch of another tree. Never can it
lean  on  a  fellow  tree  for  support.  It  stands  lone.  But  it  is
stronger  than  the  other  trees,  because  it  has  a  need  to  be.  People
too,  when  deprived  of  the  support  of  others,  grow  stronger.  Do You
plant people
away from
people to
make them
stronger?

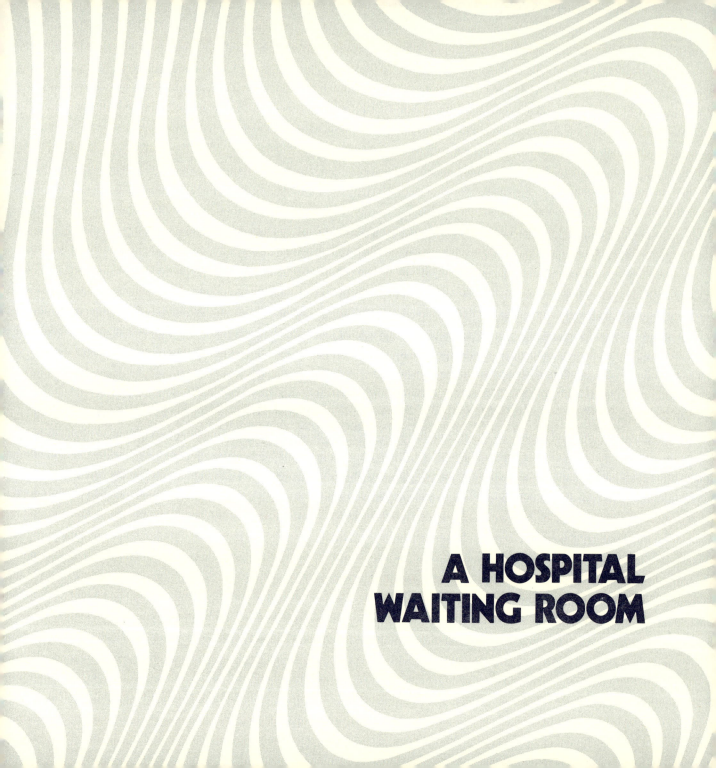

**A HOSPITAL
WAITING ROOM**

I am sitting in a hospital waiting
room. As I look upon countless faces of
distress, I wonder how many are praying,
how many have a God to pray to. I
couldn't begin to comfort one of them, if
I couldn't build from a foundation of You,
my God. And for those who don't have You
to relate to, why aren't they screaming out
with the vain emptiness of suffering? They
are strong if they can carry their grief
alone. Maybe some of them are groping in
the musty darkness of their minds now,

groping for support. Some are pleading
Your help in clumsy, unrehearsed prayer.
Some are trying to draw close to you, trying
to create a friendship that should have existed
long ago. And some are cursing You—You have up-
set their well-made plans, brought them to wait on
these worn hospital benches . . . waiting for news that
may break them up inside. God, for all who can't see that
You have a reason for everything, accept my prayer for them,
and help them even though they can't quite find You to ask You.
sorrow                                           sorrow
sorrow                                           sorrow
sorrow                                           sorrow
sorrow                                           sorrow
sorrow                                           sorrow
sorrow                                           sorrow
sorrow                                           sorrow
sorrow                                           sorrow
                                                 sorrow

THANK YOU

Thank
You,             Lord, for             show-
ing me       in a thousand       ways,
that           nothing will       ever
sat-              isfy me,          but
You. Thank You for     leaving
a trace of bitterness in every
sweet thing I seek. Thank
you for leaving me with
empty hands after
finding what I
was so sure
would satisfy.
Thank you for
letting friends
disappoint me
when I needed them
so much, because all
these things sent me to You.

A SEED INTO MY LIFE

How many times, my Divine Sower, You

d
  r
    o
     p
      a
       s
       e
       e
       d
        i
        n
        t
        o

my life,

and I fail to give it proper growing conditions. It struggles to live in torrid sun, hard ground, and distracting winds. I tremble to think how it might grow if I provided its needs: the life-giving rays of nourishing grace, the moist soil of receptivity, and the quiet restful moments for growth. The little seed could soon become like Your fruitful fig tree in the parable: a tree that invites others to come live in its branches.

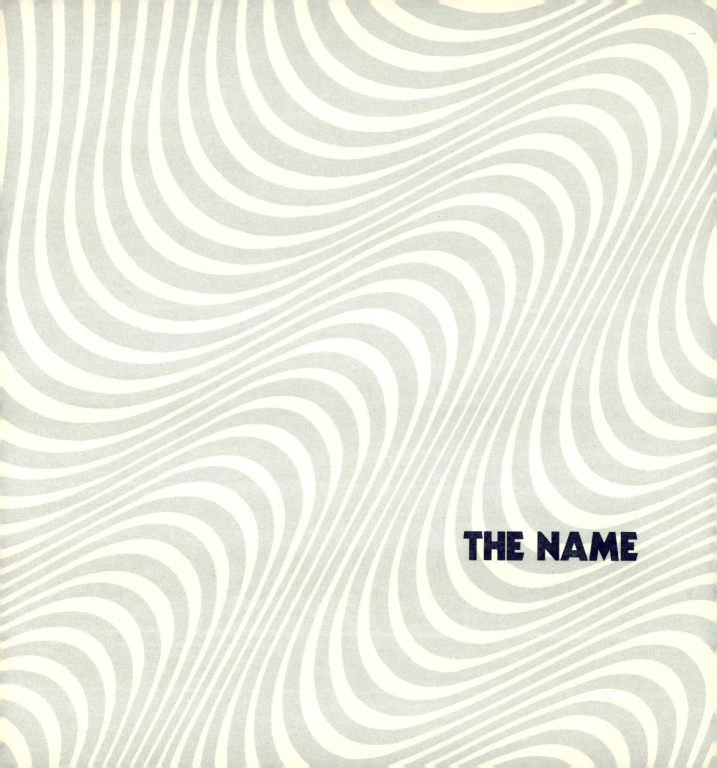

THE NAME

Jesus.                    Such
goodness I              feel, just
saying Your name.     over and over. It
is a practice that gives the commonplace moment golden importance. If the moment contains
mention of Your Holy Name, it is no longer just
a moment. It is an everlasting alleluia!  Your
name lingers in my mind like a sustained organ
chord, holding still in incensed air, en-
thralling, captivating. Your Name be-
seeched, is like a child's call for
assurance, knowing the mother is
by his side, but finding comfort  in calling. The wind
repeats  it from tree to
tree, the water from
wave to wave. As the
dark heavy night
stills the world
I hear my own
heartbeat re-
peat it like
a litany:
Jesus,
Jesus,
Jes-
us.

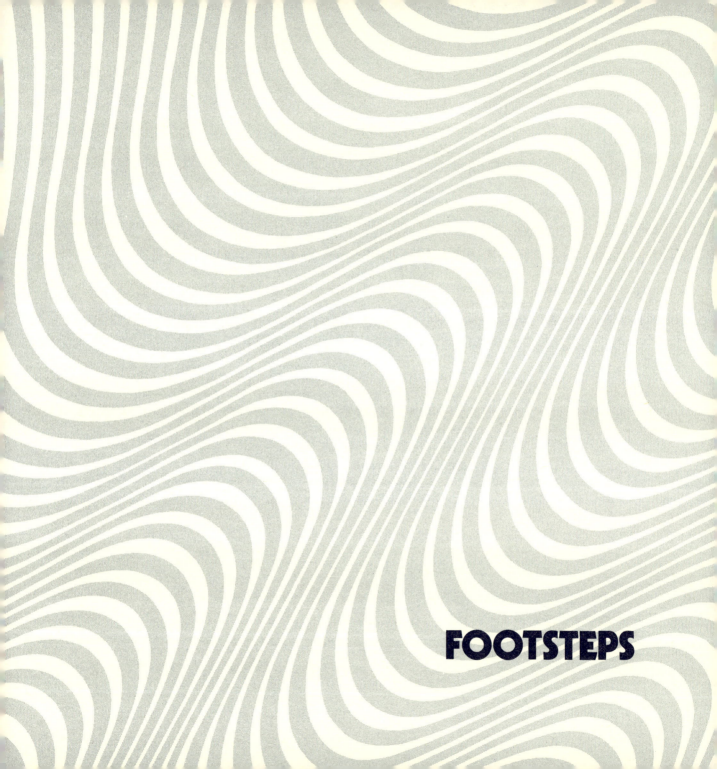

FOOTSTEPS

The stone steps
that lead to the cathedral
are worn by human feet. I
wonder how many were light, eager
feet, exultant to see the altar inside where the King of heaven and
earth abides? How many were aged
feet, shuffling, unsteady, unsure?
How many were young feet, that do
not know yet how eagerly Christ
called to them: "Suffer the
little children to come to
Me"? How many were guilty
feet that carried the dust
of sin up to the altar
where the Immaculate
Lamb of God stood in
contrast? How many
were indifferent feet,
that walked as thought-
lessly and carelessly as
if entering the city mar-
ketplace? Then how are
they different when they
walk out? Has their en-
counter with Christ changed
them? Are they more eager
to spread the Good News
of God's love, or do
they walk away aim-
lessly?

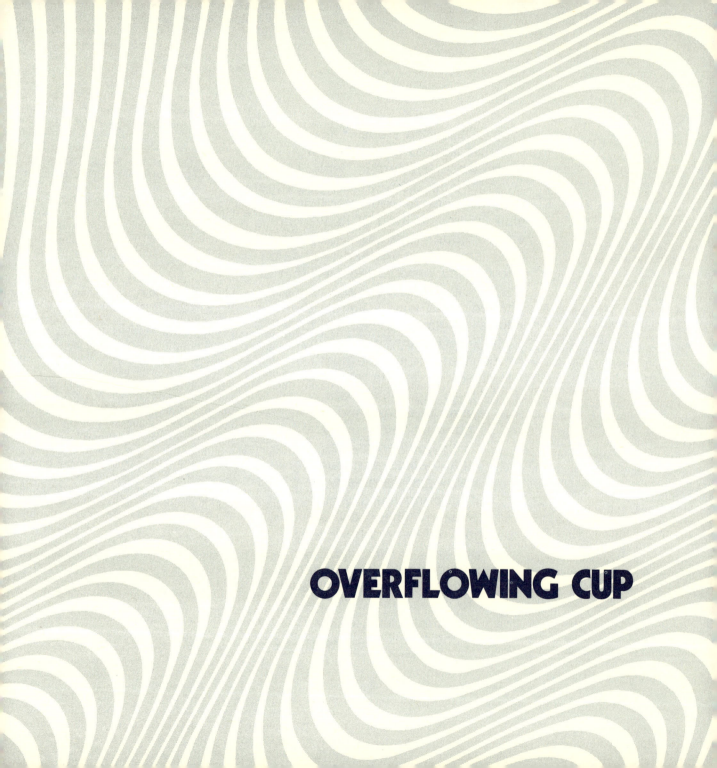

OVERFLOWING CUP

O God of silence and low voice, You will
not scream out to be heard by Your people.
If we are lost in a sea of world cacophony,
we will miss Your symphony. If we
never provide You with a quiet,
still-standing cup, how
are You to fill the
ever-moving cup
with Your
grace?
And if
the cup is
already brim-
ming over with
worldliness, how can
You fill an already full
cup? When You see an empty cup
in pleading hands, I know You cannot
pass by unmindfull of its needs. As You
pass along with Your pitcher of life-giving
grace, how heavy in Your hands it must become as
You meet cup after cup already filled, filled with
what You know will never satisfy, but will only increase thirst.
Help me, my God, to empty my cup so You may fill it with the water of life.

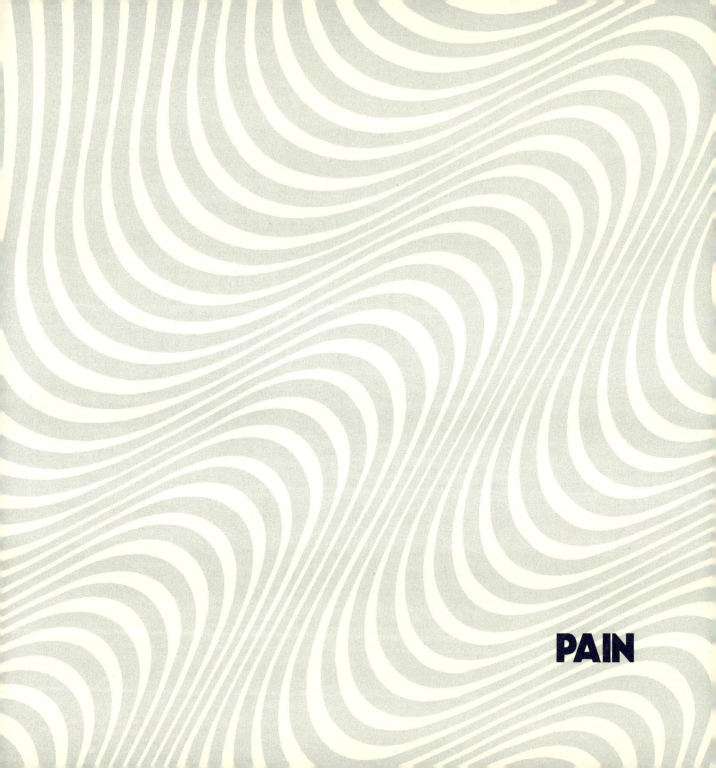

PAIN

Pain could touch our lives and create a new dimension if we didn't fight it or run from it.
We ought to relate it to the pain suffered by You, our Divine Savior.
We can compare our headache to the pulse of pain You suffered under the
crown of thorns. We can compare our backache to the strained, pulled
muscles You suffered under the weight of the cross. We can compare our
loneliness and sense of abandonment to Your forsaken heart when You
cried: "My God, My God, why have You forsaken Me?" We can compare
the infidelity of our friends to Your: "Judas, would you betray Me with
a kiss?" We can compare our rejection by friends to Peter's words
concerning You: "I swear I know Him not." My God, is there anything
I could suffer that You have not?

# TREE TURNED
# TO CROSS THAT DAY

A
tree
stands tall
and proud before
me. Think, strong
tree, you will never
have to hold a crucified
Savior. Another tree before
you was sentenced to that
role. The fiat of that tree
served, and saved you and all
other trees from serving a
Good Friday. That Good Friday Tree
with its heavy burden reached
up to heaven to hand God the
Father our atonement. You must
feel the shame that your fellow
tree felt as it held up the Savior.
And yet, you must feel the honor, too,
your fellow tree felt as it was chosen
to be a part of the Redemption.
Iron turned to nails that day;
tree turned to cross that
day all be-
cause
men
be-
came
exe-
cu-
tion-
ers
that
day.

PULSE

For one full moment, I watched the pulse beat in my wrist. If for one moment, You forgot about me, my God, and didn't generate the heartbeat, it would stop. I would be no more.

Then I think of the millions of people whose heartbeats You are generating: the pulse in the brain surgeon's hand; the pulse in the coal miner's muscled hand; the slowing-down pulse in the dying; the quickening pulse in the new-born. All of this you tend to. You kept the pulse beating in the hand that reached for thirty pieces of silver to sell You; you kept the pulse beating in the hand that held the nail for the hammer on Calvary. You kept alive the pulse of mankind that stilled yours on Good Friday. You can stop the course of blood in any of us at anytime. It seems that You would be tempted sometimes . . .

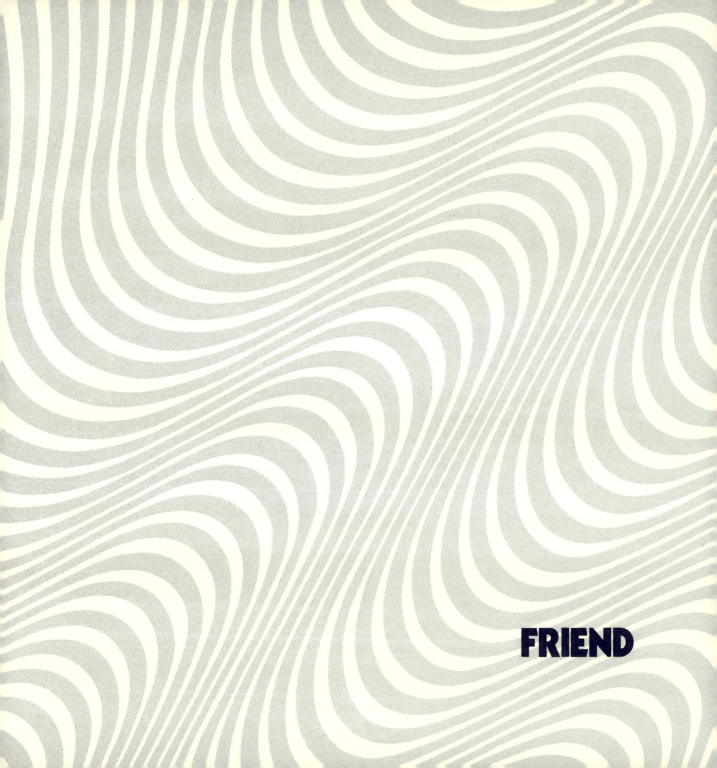

FRIEND

You came to me
today, God; I
felt Your dear
touch in the
visit of a
friend. I need-
ed what You gave
me through my
friend. I didn't          friend
feel his giving
to me, I felt
Yours. He could
not have known my
soul's needs as
he did without
divine promptings.

When life was a
single note, he
made of it a ma-
jestic chord.
When life was a
single stroke of
the artist's brush,
he made of it a
completed master-
piece. Where life
was one line of
lyric, he made of
it a magnificent
poem.

But not he . . . You.

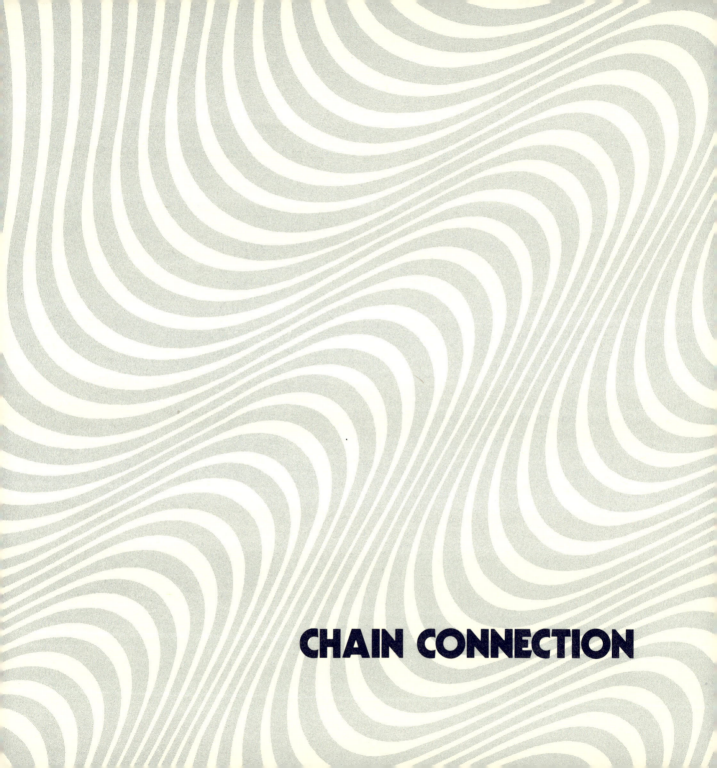

CHAIN CONNECTION

Sometimes the lonely and forgotten are so hungry for the love of someone, that they can think of nothing but ways to satisfy that pressing hunger. And most seek in vain while no one cares that they are growing more and more hungry.

Sometimes, before such souls can be brought to Your love, they must be softened by human love. Then, made susceptible to love they can feel, they can be led to Your love, the only love that satisfies but cannot always be felt.

O God, love these lonely ones through the medium of me. Let me be the link of love that will, in turn, link them directly to You. And when they are ready for a direct connection to You, quietly unfasten me from the chain.

HIS WILL

Dante said:
"In His will
is our peace."
The peace
that doing
His will
brings, is
the secret
of the monk's
devoted
strokes of
the quill,
the mystic's prayer, the mother's neat, tiny hemstitches,
the father's rhythmic tap of the hammer. The peace of
knowing one is doing God's will for the moment, is what
transforms the significant into greatness, the greatness
into worship. Whatever the work, a name printed on a
child's
kindergarten
paper, or a
signature on
a national
document,
both equally
worship the
God who as-
signed it.

Listen for the will of God in your life, my soul.

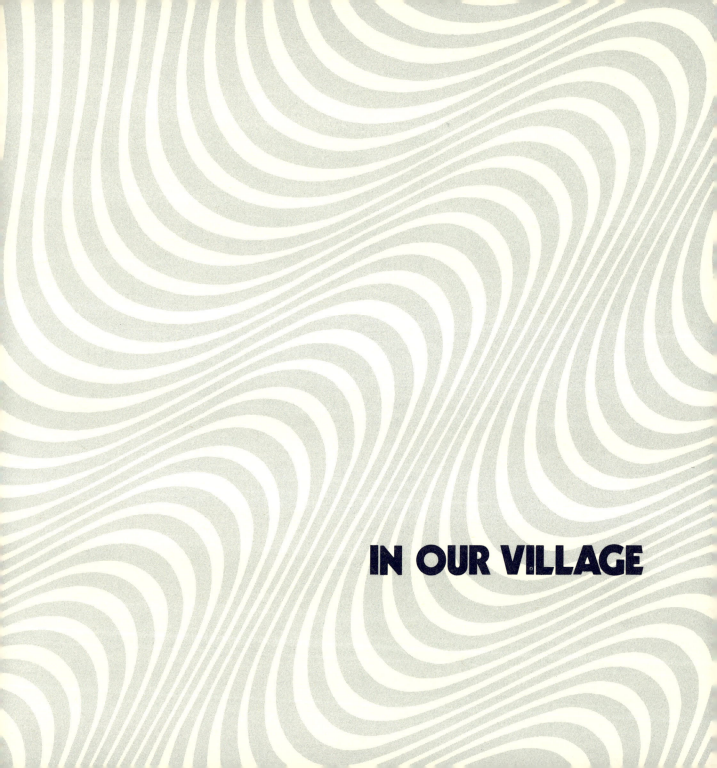

# IN OUR VILLAGE

Remember, Lord, when you were asked to spare a city if a certain number
of faithful ones could be found, and they could not be found?
What would you find under a similar assignment here today in our little
village? How many today have let one thought of You bless their minds?
How many when good fortune swept over them have referred the blessing
to You? How many have seen You in all that is happening to them
today, in all the unsolved remainders of the day? How many can still see you in their
lowest fall? Do we have any saints here in this little village who could redeem us, or have
we all left You, safe and secure, behind stained-glass chapel windows?

PRISON

O God, send Your light into my dark, deep prison of self. Just
one transcendent ray will show me that the walls I have built
around myself are penetrable by You. I am swallowed up by the
darkness I am in. My heart is pale and lifeless like a plant
that has been deprived of sunlight. Let Your light stream in

| | |
|---|---|
| while I look for | breaks in my prison walls |
| from which I might | wrest out my escape. I |
| shut myself away | from the people of Your |
| creation. I built    myself in | and other people out. I |
| thought it would be | safer, more secure. Then |
| I looked around for | You. I call out for You. |

You do not answer me. It is not at all as I expected it would
be. It is damp, void, oppressive in this darkness. I call out
for deliverance, but all I hear is the echo of my calling. I am
beginning to believe that You expect me to come out of self to
find You. With the sledgehammer of grace, tear down my walls,
and rescue me, my Deliverer.

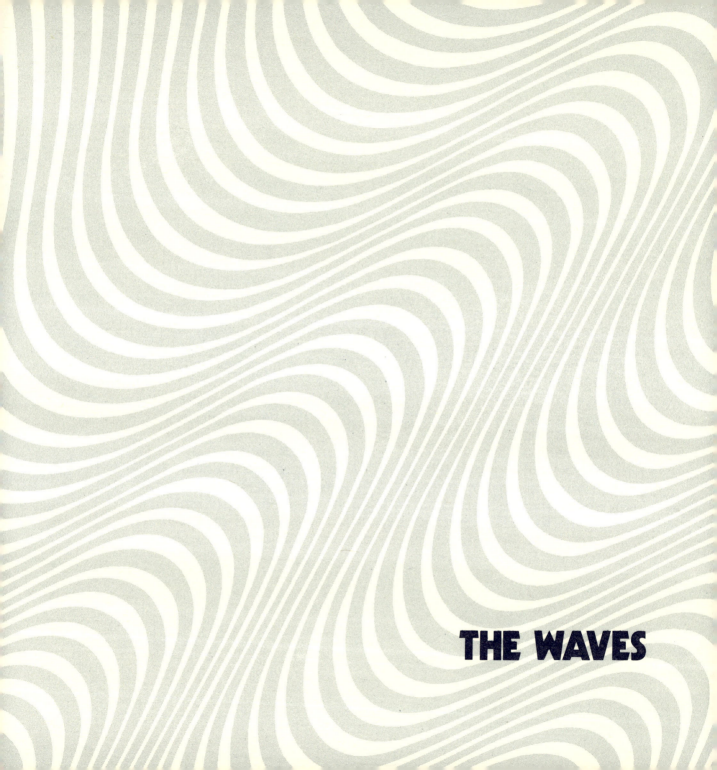

THE WAVES

An endless blue lake lies before me inviting me to rest in its blue liquid lap. I listen to the waves as they break at the shore. They say the same thing over and over again, and what is strange, whatever I ask them to say, they say. How useless to give them a silly, idle message such as blue is the sky, blue is the sky, blue is the sky. I will make them pray

Lord have mercy   Lord have mercy   Lord have mercy.

AUGUST SUNLIGHT

August sunlight catches the
corn silk, spinning the field
before me into pure gold. Early
in the cold spring, the little seeds
of corn surrendered themselves to the
tomb of heavy, moist earth. Then, urged
on my spring rains and summer sun, they
found new life by dying. Now the golden
ears nourish us as they reflect their warm
amber color on the faces of those around my
table. When winter comes the animals and the
birds will glean the field for the lingering taste
of August they will find in the stray kernels that escaped the harvester. The little seeds of corn, without dying to themselves, could not be reborn to usefulness. I, too, must die to self, if I am to be reborn to usefulness in the hands of You, O Christ. The sunlight of Your grace can spin me into pure gold.

PEACEFUL WATERS

The world offers such a cacophony of sound; help me, Lord, to maintain
a symphony of silence within. Living in the sultry heat of society, my
soul longs for cool solitude. I must retreat now and then from the world,
and nourish my soul with the sweet milk of quiet contemplation . . .
contemplation of You.
Then the peace which You help me to maintain within may o
v
e
r
f
l
o
w

and still the troubled waters
of others.

HOW DO WE
THINK OF YOU, MY GOD

God, when people think of You what aspect of You do they consider? What picture of You do they paint in their minds? You, as King of might and power, white-robed, reigning triumphantly in heaven, running things expertly but remotely? Or do they think of Your vulnerable humanity? An Infant in Bethlehem, lodged with animals and able to be made cold by night winds? A Man in the Garden of Gethsemane reduced to tears and able to be made sorrowful unto death? A Man dying on a cross unrecognizable? I think most people prefer to think of Your kingly robes, prefer to forget the blood-stained one that men cast lots over one late afternoon.

The world needs to think of You as the One who said: "Come to Me all you heavily burdened. I will give you rest . . ."

NATURE

        Nature
     never revolts
   against You, my God.
     It is always an unrippled reflection          of
  Your       will. I am here deeply shadowed in an ash      grove
  and all    is in harmony. There is a place here for every   thing. There
 is no struggling for first place. There is room for the tiny wood violet;
 there is room for the titanic rotting oak. There is room for the newborn
lamb; there is room for the aged Jersey cow. There is room for every sound:
 the timid cricket-call; the brash hawk's holler. There is room for the light
step of a frisking colt; there is room for the heavy paw of the black bear.
All sounds become orchestral parts in a pastoral overture. Soon this lively
 overture will soften to a nocturnal lullaby as the world prepares for night.
  n   Dimmer, dimmer, dimmer become the sounds.          All is
  a              whisper-soft now, and the barn owl hoots        s
  t                      the night curfew.                       t
  u                            i                                  i
  r                            s                                  l
  e       Dew tiptoes across the sleeping grass.                 l

SUNFLOWER

As the sunflower
turns to face its God
all day, I ought. I could
make of this earth a heaven
if I could learn to keep facing
the Light, the Way, and the Truth.
The clouds of my earth-centered life come
between me and my God, and the whole
day passes without sight or thought
of Him. I am getting rather used
to this grayness of life without my sun. Day by day, I
am forgetting more and
more what it is like
to see the sun.
O
G
o
d
break through
the
clouds
of
self-
centeredness,
and
show
me
You.

WHAT WAS IT LIKE?

What
was
it
like
be-
neath
the
cross
on the afternoon You died, O Lord? Did
Your faithful ones kneel close enough to
You
to
hear
Your
chok-
ing
breaths?
Could
they
see
the
pain
twist
Your
Body?
Did they see Your redeeming Blood r i
v
e
r
e d  in the sand?

PRAISE

Praise be to God in the thunder
of the storm; praise be to God
in the hush of the morn.

Praise be to God in the sway
of the willow; praise be to God
in the straight of the pine.

Praise be to God in the fragrance
of the rose; praise be to God in the
hurt of the thorn.

Praise be to God in sunlight over
sand; praise be to God in moonlight
over water.

Praise be to God in the warmth
of together; praise be to God
in the chill of alone.

Praise be to God in the plenty
of His Presence; praise be to
God in the empty of His Absence.

STAR

In
this
quiet
night as
I look into the heavens, it seems there
are only stars and me. I stand facing
up to the truth of the stars, and
the world around me seems
unreal. I feel one with
the stars, distant though
they be. There's a part of them
reflected in me.   They twinkle in
a vastness that    holds them off
from me. I          live in  a
vastness              that , too,
iso-                      lates me.


As I reach for stars forever beyond reach . . .
    so I reach for God . . .  too, forever beyond reach . . .

FRIENDSHIP

I
touched the
friendship,          oh,
so lightly at        first,
all was dis-         covery,
experiment,      and new!
My heart      quickened at
the sight of my friend,
thrilled, excited, in
silent empathy.
I gathered
thoughts to
hold in memory
to sustain longing
absences between.
Then slyly the light-
ness that made our hearts
sing became weighted down
with the heavy hand of time.
All areas surveyed, no fields
left untilled. And the friendship
sadly starved itself away, away.
But, my God, a friendship with
You is everlasting because the rich-
ness of You is endless.

JOY

Joy is                  dancing
in my heart             like a nodding
daffodil; joy               is loud in my
heart like a thundering waterfall.
Joy is quiet in my heart like a
whisper of stars; joy is feeling one with creation. Joy
is flaming with the sun;
joy is drifting with
the clouds; joy is sway-
ing with the willow, joy is
lapping with the waves. Joy is
feeling one with creation. Joy
is being in    j  tune with You,
God. Joy       o  is being one
with           y        God.
               j
               o
               y
               j
               o
               y
               j
               o
               y

# THE WIND
# HAS MANY FACES

The wind has many faces. When I am laughing, it carries my laughter and ripples the fields into smiles. When I am crying, it dries my tears into nothingness. When I am empty of thought, it fills my mind with a symphony of sound. It adds fear to a stormy night, and brings humanity close together. The most comfortable face of you, O wind, is your lullably at night, your gentle rap on the window, as you sing alto with the
willow bough.